CARRIE
CHAPMAN CATT
A VOICE FOR WOMEN

SPECIAL LIVES IN HISTORY THAT BECOME

Signature LIVES

CARRIE
CHAPMAN CATT
A VOICE FOR WOMEN

by Kristin Thoennes Keller

Content Adviser: Martha Gardner, Ph.D.,
Assistant Professor, Department of History,
DePaul University

Reading Adviser: Rosemary G. Palmer, Ph.D.,
Department of Literacy, College of Education,
Boise State University

COMPASS POINT BOOKS MINNEAPOLIS, MINNESOTA

Compass Point Books
151 Good Counsel Drive
P.O. Box 669
Mankato, MN 56002-0669

Visit Compass Point Books on the Internet at *www.compasspointbooks.com*
or e-mail your request to *custserv@compasspointbooks.com*.

Editor: Jennifer VanVoorst
Lead Designer: Jaime Martens
Photo Researcher: Marcie C. Spence
Page Production: Heather Griffin
Cartographer: XNR Productions, Inc.
Educational Consultant: Diane Smolinski

Managing Editor: Catherine Neitge
Creative Director: Keith Griffin
Editorial Director: Carol Jones

Library of Congress Cataloging-in-Publication Data
Thoennes Keller, Kristin.
  Carrie Chapman Catt: a voice for women / by Kristin Thoennes Keller.
    p. cm. — (Signature lives.)
  Includes bibliographical references and index.
  ISBN-13: 978-0-7565-0991-0 (hardcover)
  ISBN-10: 0-7565-0991-2 (hardcover)
  1. Catt, Carrie Chapman, 1859–1947. 2. National American Woman
Suffrage Association. 3. Suffragists—United States—Biography. I. Title.
II. Series.
JK1899.C3T56 2006
324.6'23'092—dc22   2005002791

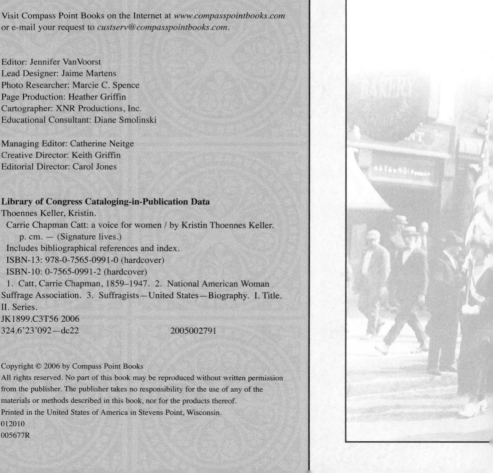

MODERN AMERICA

Starting in the late 19th century, advancements in all areas of human activity transformed an old world into a new and modern place. Inventions prompted rapid shifts in lifestyle, and scientific discoveries began to alter the way humanity viewed itself. Beginning with World War I, warfare took place on a global scale, and ideas such as nationalism and communism showed that countries were taking a larger view of their place in the world. The combination of all these changes continues to produce what we know as the modern world.

Table of Contents

1 THE FIGHT FOR THE RIGHT

❧⟳❧

Carrie Chapman Catt made her choice and marked her ballot. This day, she must have thought, was surely one of the proudest of her life. Catt had spent decades lobbying state and federal governments to pass a women's suffrage amendment, a law that would grant women a right they had long been denied. Now, on November 2, 1920, millions of American women crowded polling places to take advantage of what Catt had worked so hard to help them gain—the right to vote.

Looking back on her nearly 40-year struggle for women's suffrage, Catt said that she became a suffragist when she was just 13 years old. Watching her father and another man prepare to go to town in order to vote in the 1872 presidential election, Carrie

During the American Revolution, women began to take on jobs that had traditionally belonged to men, including, in some cases, fighting.

turned to her mother and asked why she wasn't changing her clothes. Her mother replied that she wasn't going. Surprised, Carrie asked her how, then, she intended to vote. Everyone present laughed out loud.

Carrie did not laugh. She was bewildered and upset by her new knowledge of politics. She had actively followed the presidential race between Horace Greeley and Ulysses S. Grant. She attended meetings and campaigned with her parents in their Iowa community. Carrie could not believe that women were not allowed to vote along with men. Carrie's outrage marked the beginning of her life-long crusade for women's suffrage, or women's right to vote. She would spend most of her adult life working tirelessly for the cause.

Concern for women's suffrage started long before Carrie came into the picture, however. In early America, women had few rights. In the late 1700s, a married woman was thought of as her husband's property. Husbands owned their wives' belongings, land, and money. Women did not control their own lives and had little control over the lives of their children. If a couple divorced, the woman lost all rights to her children.

At the end of the 18th century, however, the Revolutionary War broke out between the American colonies and Great Britain. While male colonists fought against Great Britain, women began doing what had been thought of as men's work. Women farmed, hunted, trapped, and ran businesses. Some women even took part in the fighting. After the colonies won their independence, women began to demand the same rights as men. One of those rights was suffrage, or the right to vote.

In 1848, Lucretia Mott and Elizabeth Cady Stanton organized a convention in Seneca Falls, New York, to talk about women's rights. The two women wrote a list of women's demands based on the Declaration of Independence. It was called the Declaration of Sentiments. The Declaration of Sentiments asserted women's right to a career and

Elizabeth Cady Stanton, one of the early founders of the women's movement, spoke at the Seneca Falls convention.

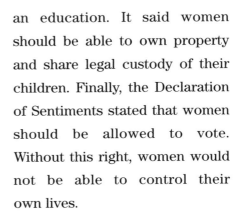

The Declaration of Sentiments asserted that women were entitled to the same rights as men because they were in fact equal to men: "Resolved, That woman is man's equal—was intended to be so by the Creator, and the highest good of the race demands that she should be recognized as such."

an education. It said women should be able to own property and share legal custody of their children. Finally, the Declaration of Sentiments stated that women should be allowed to vote. Without this right, women would not be able to control their own lives.

Sixty-eight women and 32 men signed the Declaration of Sentiments in support. The convention angered many people, but it motivated women all over the United States to organize their own meetings about women's suffrage.

Women who were interested in reform in the 1800s took many risks. It was new for women to speak in public. Those who did often were pelted with rocks and eggs. Buildings where they spoke were sometimes burned. But the women persevered in many reforms.

Eventually, the original suffrage leaders grew too old to continue their fight, and they passed the torch to other dedicated suffragists. In 1890, Carrie Chapman Catt gave a speech at the convention of the National American Woman Suffrage Association (NAWSA). Those who heard her said

UNITED STATES POSTAGE

ELIZABETH STANTON   CARRIE C. CATT   LUCRETIA MOTT

3¢   100 YEARS OF PROGRESS   3¢
1848   OF WOMEN   1948

she was magnetic in her ability to command the full attention of the crowd. The aging suffrage leaders knew Catt had what it took to keep the movement going.

Catt, born 11 years after the Seneca Falls convention, became president of NAWSA in 1900. Lobbying governments, giving speeches, and organizing others, Catt worked tirelessly to achieve the result none of the original leaders lived long enough to see: women's suffrage. ℘

In 1948, the U.S. Postal Service issued a stamp honoring Catt and the organizers of the Seneca Falls convention.

13

2 BORN TO LEAD

❧❦❧

Carrie Chapman Catt was born Carrie Clinton Lane on January 9, 1859, on a family farm in Ripon, Wisconsin. She was the middle of three children born to Lucius and Maria Clinton Lane.

Stories about Carrie's childhood suggest she was born to be a leader and a crusader for gender equality. She was organized, intelligent, and rational. Once, when her older brother chased her with a snake, she ran away screaming. Then she stopped herself. If the snake was not harming Charles, she reasoned, then it wouldn't harm her either. She caught the snake, waited until Charles wasn't expecting it, and wrapped the thing around his neck.

Carrie's first experience in defending her own gender came at the early age of 6. As she described

Carrie Lane was one of the first women in the nation to be appointed superintendent of schools.

it, she and her first-grade classmates

> *were lined up with our toes touching one straight crack. Suddenly, while the teacher was talking to us, one of the girls' hoopskirts became loose and slipped to the ground. The little girl blushed and the boys all began to giggle out loud. The teacher tactfully gathered up the girl and her hoopskirt, and repaired the damage. At noontime those boys came to the girl and poked fun at her, and as they continued their annoyance, I went up to the leader and slapped his face! They had more respect for us girls after that!*

Carrie had authority with other children in the classroom as well. In the one-room schoolhouses of those days, older children often were asked to help younger children. Because she was both clever and good at explaining ideas, Carrie's teachers often asked her to help other children with their studies. Later in life, Carrie would spend a great deal of time speaking publicly, and her success at it probably had its roots in her early educational experiences.

Carrie also was very organized as a child. Whenever she was given chores, she broke down her work into manageable chunks. She managed her schoolwork and chores with little effort. All of these organizational skills would serve her well when she led the women's suffrage movement.

When Carrie was 7, her family moved from Wisconsin to Charles City, Iowa. There, she attended the one-room schoolhouse down the road until it was time for her to go to the high school in town. In good weather, she rode her horse the five miles (eight kilometers) from the farm to school each day. In winter, she stayed with friends. They later remembered her as a clever and lively houseguest.

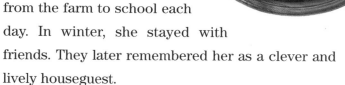

Even as a child, Carrie looked out for her own gender.

Early in her teen years, Carrie decided she wanted to become a doctor, even though few women in those days practiced medicine. She was interested in all living things and studied the reptiles and insects she brought into the home. Lizards crawled around. Butterflies emerged from cocoons. Carrie collected the brains from various dead animals and kept them in jars and bottles. If live specimens died, she would preserve them in her mother's canning jars. Her parents tolerated all of this until Carrie brought in a batch of rattlesnake

Carrie's childhood home in Charles City, Iowa, was known as Spring Brook Farm.

eggs. Her father destroyed them in the kitchen stove.

Carrie's interests grew as she did, and she soon was reading a copy of Charles Darwin's *The Origin of Species*. While she later admitted to not understanding much of it, she began asking difficult questions about Earth, science, and God. Even as a teenager, Carrie was interested in thinking about ideas in new ways, in ways that challenged the common assumptions. College was the natural next step for her.

She approached her father during her junior year in high school with information about Iowa State Agricultural College (now Iowa State University). This school had opened in 1869 in Ames. Tuition was free, meals were $2.50 a week, and a room in the dormitory cost anywhere from $1 to $3.50 per term. Students could make it on $150 a year, but Carrie's father was a farmer and had little money to spare. He offered to pay $25 per year and told her she would have to earn the rest.

Lucius was surprised when Carrie told him that she already had it covered. She planned to teach during the summers. Since the Civil War, most teachers were young, single women who were paid about $26 per month and were required to resign when they got married. Also, as more and more country schools opened, the state found itself with a shortage of teachers.

Carrie Lane entered Iowa State Agricultural College in March 1877. She washed dishes for 9 cents an hour during her first two years. After that, she worked in the library, a job that other students envied because it paid the top student wage of 10 cents per hour. And on college breaks, Carrie taught in the country schools.

Carrie discovered her gift for public speaking while giving a speech during her first year in college. She was only 18 years old, but Carrie's

Iowa State Agricultural College was housed in a single Victorian building. Carrie's class was only the ninth in the college's short history. Six of the 27 students who started along with Carrie were women. She earned A's and B's during her years there. Carrie was the only woman among the 18 graduates at the commencement ceremony of November 10, 1880.

comments caused enough of a stir that she was quoted in her hometown newspaper. She was explaining why women should have a right to an education and said that educated women would be able to bring up their children well. Carrie then related her ideas to women's suffrage, arguing against the common idea that women were not intelligent enough to vote. She concluded her argument by asking, "How is it possible that a woman who is unfit to vote, should be the mother of, and bring up, a man who is?"

Carrie looked out for women's interests in other ways while still in college. Once, she heard a military training officer speak about the healthy aspects of military drill exercises. Carrie knew that the male students took part in the drills, and she questioned why women students did not have such training. She went on to start the Ladies Military Company, known as G Company (G for Girls), which drilled with broomsticks. The college maintained G Company until 1897, when it was replaced by physical education.

During her second year of college, Carrie also

won the right for women to speak in the Crescent Literary Society. In this organization, men were given a topic on which to speak, without preparation, for three minutes. This skill was supposed to help them develop quick thinking and self-confidence. Women who participated, however, were only allowed to write essays on topics and then read them aloud. Carrie, frustrated, finally had enough. She challenged this policy by speaking out of turn on the topic of women's suffrage. From then on, she held offices in the Crescent Literary Society. In doing so, she learned the parliamentary procedure. This method of conducting meetings is one she would use to lead meetings throughout the world all her life.

Carrie graduated from college in 1880 and worked briefly as a law clerk before becoming a teacher in the Mason City, Iowa, school system. By 1883, she had become superintendent of the schools in Mason City, an unusual achievement for a woman in those days. She resigned from that position in 1885 to marry Leo Chapman because women were expected to stop working when they married. Carrie did not stop working altogether, however. She worked alongside her husband, who was the editor and publisher of the *Mason City Republican* newspaper. Only one month after their marriage, a new section called "Woman's World" appeared in the paper. Carrie was the author. Instead of discussing fashion styles or food, however, she wrote about more serious issues for women, including women's suffrage.

In May 1886, the Chapmans decided to move to San Francisco, California. Leo went ahead to find work, but in less than a year, he became ill with typhoid fever. Carrie was on her way to California by train when she learned that Leo had died. Within a few months, Carrie had lost her income, her home, her husband, and the newspaper.

San Francisco of the late 19th century was a bustling port city.

After Leo's death, Carrie stayed in San Francisco and lived with an aunt. Her life there was difficult. Instead of going back to teaching, she sold newspaper advertising and wrote articles as the city's first female newspaper reporter. Carrie worked hard, but she never knew from job to job whether she'd get another assignment and be able to earn more money. Even worse, a male co-worker once made unwanted advances toward Carrie, and she had to fight him off. Carrie understood what it was like to be a working woman, and she became determined to do something for women's protection. She believed even then that women's suffrage was the answer. ❧

3 THE SUFFRAGE MOVEMENT

❧

Carrie Chapman Catt lived during a time of tremendous social change. People were working to fix society's problems through reform movements. The three main reform movements of the 1800s were temperance, abolition, and women's suffrage. Each concerned women, but in very different ways.

The temperance movement was a national effort to stop the manufacture and sale of alcoholic drinks. Alcohol contributed to many social problems. Many men drank up all their wages. As a result, their families went without necessary items. Other men used violence against women while under the influence of alcohol. Temperance activists believed that the problems associated with drinking alcohol would be solved if alcohol were prohibited. Many

Elizabeth Cady Stanton (left) and Susan B. Anthony were two of the founders and driving forces behind the women's suffrage movement.

women supported prohibition.

Abolition was an antislavery movement. Its goals varied from group to group. Some wanted to end slavery altogether. Others wanted simply to stop the spread of slavery into new U.S. territories. Many people saw the abolitionists' aims as closely linked with the suffrage movement since both slaves and women lacked the legal freedoms that white men enjoyed.

The third major reform movement was women's suffrage, officially begun in 1848 at the Seneca Falls convention. In 1869, however, the women's suffrage movement split into two separate groups over the issue of whether to support black suffrage. One group, led by Lucy Stone, was called the American Women's Suffrage Association (AWSA). This group wanted moral reform in general and didn't focus exclusively on women's right to vote. The other group, called the National Woman Suffrage Association (NWSA), was led by Susan B. Anthony and Elizabeth Cady Stanton. This group wanted to work only on votes for women and not on other reforms.

In 1890, the two suffrage organizations united under the name of the National American Woman Suffrage Association (NAWSA). This group's only concern was women's suffrage. The new organization's first president was Elizabeth Cady Stanton, followed by Susan B. Anthony. Eventually, Carrie would follow Anthony as the group's third president, but a lot happened from the time Carrie lost her husband and the time she led the suffrage movement.

During the year she lived in San Francisco, Carrie met a man named George Catt. He remembered her as a fellow student from Iowa State Agricultural College in Ames. George was living in San Francisco and worked as a civil engineer at a bridge-building firm. He was good at his work, handsome, and unmarried. He and Carrie became friends.

Some sources say that it was probably George who encouraged Carrie to begin a career as a public speaker.

Elizabeth Cady Stanton, one of the founders of the women's suffrage movement, became interested in the cause through her abolitionist work. While attending an antislavery convention, she was shocked to find that not only were women not allowed to be delegates, but that they also had to watch the proceedings from behind a curtain. This unfairness prompted Stanton to take up the cause of women's rights, including women's suffrage.

She realized she could make more money speaking than selling advertising for newspapers. Soon Carrie had written and delivered three lectures. Her speeches centered on political topics such as immigration. They showed her ability to think through complicated issues. The lectures were popular with audiences who supported women's rights.

After polishing and practicing her speeches on the West Coast, Carrie moved back to Charles City,

Iowa, in August 1887. Lecturing was a difficult lifestyle. Carrie spent many nights away from home, she often missed meals, and she spent long hours on trains. But her new career paid well. Carrie earned more than $100 in the first four months. She paid $10 a month for her house in Charles City. With the rest of the money, she had to pay for food, heat, and other necessary items. Her life was better than the one she'd had in San Francisco, but it was not in any way luxurious.

Carrie also took on other tasks during this time. She looked after her younger brother, Will, who lived with her. She edited the *Floyd County Advocate* for a few months. And she worked for the Woman's Christian Temperance Union (WCTU).

The same year that Carrie moved back to Iowa, the U.S. Senate voted on a proposed amendment to allow women's suffrage, but the amendment did not pass. After that, the suffragists decided to develop strong local suffrage groups around the country that would work for suffrage on a state-by-state basis.

Two years later, Iowa was one of the states pushing for suffrage. In October 1889, Carrie attended the Iowa suffrage convention and was made recording secretary. When Lucy Stone heard Carrie speak, she said, "Mrs. Chapman will be heard from yet in this movement." Carrie was unanimously elected lecturer and organizer for the Iowa suffrage

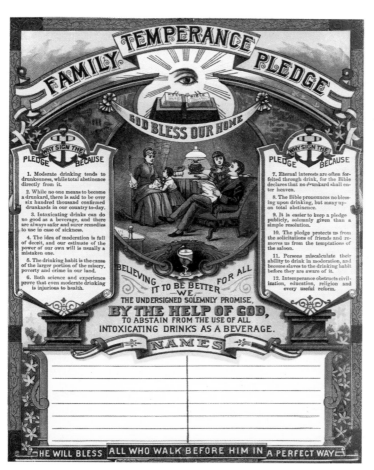

FAMILY TEMPERANCE PLEDGE

GOD BLESS OUR HOME

WHY SIGN THE PLEDGE BECAUSE

1. Moderate drinking tends to drunkenness, while total abstinence directly from it.

2. While no one means to become a drunkard, there is said to be over six hundred thousand confirmed drunkards in our country to-day.

3. Intoxicating drinks can do no good as a beverage, and there are always safer and surer remedies to use in case of sickness.

4. The idea of moderation is full of deceit, and our estimate of the power of our own will is usually a mistaken one.

5. The drinking habit is the cause of the larger portion of the misery, poverty and crime in our land.

6. Both science and experience prove that even moderate drinking is injurious to health.

WHY SIGN THE PLEDGE BECAUSE

7. Eternal interests are often forfeited through drink, for the Bible declares that no drunkard shall enter heaven.

8. The Bible pronounces no blessing upon drinking, but many upon total abstinence.

9. It is easier to keep a pledge publicly, solemnly given than a simple resolution.

10. The pledge protects us from the solicitations of friends and removes us from the temptations of the saloon.

11. Persons miscalculate their ability to drink in moderation, and become slaves to the drinking habit before they are aware of it.

12. Intemperance obstructs civilization, education, religion and every useful reform.

BELIEVING IT TO BE BETTER FOR ALL
—WE—
THE UNDERSIGNED SOLEMNLY PROMISE,
BY THE HELP OF GOD,
TO ABSTAIN FROM THE USE OF ALL
INTOXICATING DRINKS AS A BEVERAGE.

NAMES

HE WILL BLESS ALL WHO WALK BEFORE HIM IN A PERFECT WAY

Organizations such as the Woman's Christian Temperance Union used religion to promote temperance.

movement. She earned a small salary traveling from town to town to gather and organize support for the cause. Within a few weeks, she started a Political Equality Club in Sioux City, Iowa. She also set up a system for collecting money in support of the group's needs. By the end of the year, Carrie had created 10 new suffrage clubs. She—and the movement—were off and running.

> *Although Carrie would later move away and live in other states, she always felt that Iowa was her home. Carrie kept in close contact with the suffragists in Iowa. She knew it was difficult for supporters in the Midwest to get all the way to Washington, D.C., for the national conference. Therefore, she organized the first Mississippi Valley Conference, which met for four days in September 1892. Carrie realized the importance of getting women together to talk about concerns, ideas, and experiences.*

For her work in Iowa, Carrie received recognition from the movement leaders, and their praise fueled her energy and dedication. She attended the 1890 NAWSA national convention in Washington, D.C. All the major leaders of women's suffrage were there: Lucy Stone, Alice Stone Blackwell, Elizabeth Cady Stanton, and Susan B Anthony. They heard Carrie's speech, called "The Symbol of Liberty." They were impressed with her words, and even more impressed with her ability to capture and hold the crowd's attention. Stanton, Anthony, and the other suffrage leaders were eager for Carrie to play a larger role in the suffrage movement.

Shortly after the national convention, Carrie left for a speaking tour to the Northwest. While in Seattle, she privately married George Catt on June 10, 1890, three years after meeting him again in San Francisco. Carrie's marriage surprised and angered other suffragists. They thought her marriage meant she would stop working. But her marriage was not conventional, nor was her new husband. Carrie wrote this of her relationship with her new husband:

> *We made a team to work for the cause. My husband used to say that he was as much a reformer as I, but that he couldn't work at reforming and earn a living at the same time; but what he could do was to earn living enough for two and free me from all economic burden, and thus I could reform for two. That was our bargain and we happily understood each other.*

A few months after settling into married life in Seattle, Carrie Chapman Catt traveled to South Dakota as a NAWSA representative. She hoped to help the state pass a referendum on women's suffrage. Catt and other suffragists had a lot to deal with in South Dakota; there was a drought, record-setting heat, and a plague of grasshoppers, as well as a lack of funding. Catt urged supporters from her hometown to distribute little pockets in which a penny a day might be collected for the cause.

The plan was to pepper the state with speakers. Catt was one of a dozen such speakers. She reported that her audiences were made up mostly of farmers who were enthusiastic for women's suffrage. Catt was impressed with the tough farm women who wanted the right to vote. Many of them were independent farmers who were widows or unmarried. The campaign was challenging, but Catt took it all in stride. She wrote of the experience,

At one place where I took three meals I had bread and watermelon and tea for each meal and the people themselves had not had anything else for a long time. I was once one of nine people sleeping in one room.

By the end of the 19th century, the United States, once a nation of farms, shops, and mills, was becoming a booming industrial power with factories that needed workers. Many immigrants came to the United States in search of a better life for themselves and their families. Beginning in 1890, the United States experienced a massive wave of immigration. By 1910, New York City had more Italians than Rome, Italy, and more Irish than Dublin, Ireland.

Despite her enthusiasm, Catt was also discouraged. She knew there were groups who did not want women's suffrage passed. Some people who opposed it simply didn't want change. Others were opposed because they disagreed with the temperance movement. They believed that if women were allowed to vote, all women would vote for prohibition of alcohol.

These people resorted to dishonesty to keep women's suffrage from being passed in South Dakota that year. Catt watched on election day as young men brought Russian-German immigrants with them to the polls. The immigrants could not read, so the young men marked the ballots for them. Of course, they marked against suffrage.

Catt was not optimistic about the outcome in South Dakota. She said, "Ours is a cold, lonesome little movement, which will make our hearts ache about November 5." Her prediction came true. The vote had been 45,862 against suffrage and 22,072 for.

Despite losing the battle in South Dakota, Catt was at the Kansas suffrage convention in a few weeks with Anthony and others who had been in South Dakota. Catt also completed her work in Iowa as she had promised to do and attended the Iowa State convention. She went home to Seattle for the holidays exhausted.

Catt was scheduled to speak at the NAWSA national convention in Washington, D.C., in February. She was on her way there when she came down with typhoid fever, the same disease that had killed her first husband less than five years earlier. For two months, she hovered between life and death. In her delirium, she recited her speeches from the South Dakota campaign over and over again. It took her months to regain her full health.

Once she was well enough, Catt began to consider ways she could help improve the suffrage organization. She thought about the lessons she had learned from the South Dakota campaign. Meanwhile, George's business took them to the East Coast. They moved to Boston, near Lucy Stone and Henry Blackwell. Catt admired and befriended Lucy Stone and her daughter Alice Stone Blackwell. Lucy was no longer actively involved in the suffrage movement because of her age. Alice had taken over editing the *Woman's Journal*, the magazine Lucy had started in order to support the earlier AWSA.

Published from 1870 to 1917, the Woman's Journal *was an important publication of the women's movement.*

At the 1892 NAWSA national convention, Elizabeth Cady Stanton and Lucy Stone retired as president and vice president. Susan B. Anthony took over as the new president. She was 73 years old. Because of her age, younger suffragists often helped her. One of those helpers was Carrie Chapman Catt.

At one point during the convention, Anthony asked Catt to accompany her to congressional hearings, where Anthony spoke and testified on the suffrage amendment. Catt was surprised when Anthony called on her to speak first. Her speech drew on Herbert Spencer, an English poet who accorded the same rights to men and women. When she was finished, she sat down and observed the rest of the hearings. She watched the politicians' lack of interest in the women's speeches and decided that something had to be done.

Anthony knew Catt had strong organizational skills. Therefore, she made Catt responsible for recruiting and educating suffragists for NAWSA. Catt hired speakers, planned their trips, made local arrangements, and raised money. She also wrote detailed instructions for starting new suffrage clubs and maintaining enthusiasm for them. She made suggestions for state meeting agendas and for the clubs' year-long plans.

The year 1893 brought the Columbian Exposition in Chicago, which opened with a

Congress of Representative Women of All Lands. The sight of women from other parts of the world stirred something in Catt, and she began to extend her concerns to women of the world, not just the women of her own country.

All the major leaders of the suffrage movement spoke. Catt herself spoke, tying in suffrage with the idea of evolution. Her speech resonated with the attendees, who were primarily educated middle-class women who had the time, energy, and money to devote to the cause.

Catt also noticed a change in the attitude of the press at the exposition. She observed that previous cartoons had shown suffragists as having escaped from mental institutions, while anti-suffrage women were always drawn as good-looking and fashionably dressed. After the convention, the cartoonists changed their depiction of suffragists. The press finally saw reformers as part of the normal American political landscape.

At the exposition, Catt was asked to help campaign in Colorado, where a small group of suffragists had quietly introduced a women's suffrage bill into the Colorado legislature. The bill had passed. The suffragists now needed money and advice to get it passed by the voters in a referendum. The task was especially challenging because it wasn't an election year. That meant that the

A political cartoon shows how many Americans of the time viewed the suffragists.

opposition would have time to actively campaign against suffrage. Susan B. Anthony said that all NAWSA's money was tied up in a Kansas campaign and would not help.

Catt decided to help anyway. She knew that Colorado had been in a financial depression. Voters would be looking for a change. The time was right, and Catt had a plan. She went about raising money for the campaign.

From the time she arrived in Colorado in early September through the next two months,

Catt traveled more than 1,000 miles (1,600 km). She visited 29 of Colorado's 63 counties. She organized 50 suffrage clubs, some of which included influential men.

Some of Catt's experiences in Colorado were as difficult as they had been in South Dakota. She was never sure who, if anyone, would show up at lectures. Travel was difficult as well. Once, because of a train wreck, she could not make one of her speaking engagements. A man with one arm offered to get her there with a handcar on the tracks. Catt climbed into the handcar and was off for a wild and windy ride. She didn't arrive at her speaking engagement until 9 P.M. The audience had been waiting for her a long time. Although she hadn't eaten anything since breakfast, Catt spoke to the eager crowd. Later, after a steak dinner, she was able to find a few hours for sleep before rising to catch a 4 A.M. train.

But all of Catt's hard work in Colorado paid off. Women's suffrage was approved on November 7, 1893, by more than 6,000 votes. Of all the counties Catt had visited, only three voted against suffrage.

Catt attributed the success in Colorado to many things. First was Colorado's closeness to Wyoming, the only other state that allowed women to vote. A few speakers from Wyoming had come to testify during the campaign. Also, the mining unions in Colorado believed in equal rights for women and

Women in Wyoming were able to vote in the presidential election of 1888.

voted to support those rights. But the main thing that helped women's suffrage pass in Colorado that year was Catt herself, along with 25 or so local suffragists who had all worked tirelessly. Catt said afterward that she felt "like a frog that had fallen into a milk pail and struggled until it had churned a fine pot of butter."

FRANK LESLIE'S
ILLUSTRATED
WEEKLY

Vol. LXXVIII—No. 2016.
Copyright, 1894, by Arkell Weekly Co.
All Rights Reserved.

NEW YORK, MAY 3, 1894.

[PRICE, 10 CENTS. $4.00 Year
12 Weeks

THE WOMAN-SUFFRAGE MOVEMENT IN NEW YORK CITY.

SOCIETY LEADERS SECURING SIGNATURES TO PETITIONS TO BE PRESENTED TO THE CONSTITUTIONAL CONVENTION—SCENE AT SHERRY'S.
DRAWN BY B. WEST CLINEDINST.—[SEE PAGE 290.]

4 PREPARING FOR LEADERSHIP

❧❦❧

After the Colorado victory, NAWSA planned its first campaign of 1894 in New York. There, a new state constitution was being considered, and the group wanted women's suffrage to be included in it. Catt gave more than 40 speeches that spring and continued to organize more suffrage groups. She found support in farmer and labor unions.

But the opposition was strong. There were, of course, those who feared prohibition. Other opponents argued that the Bible stated that women were inferior to men and so should not be given the same rights. Some people argued that the right to vote carried with it the obligation to carry arms, which women were not allowed to do. Still others even claimed that women didn't really want to vote.

New York City suffragists collected signatures on petitions to be presented at the 1894 state constitutional convention.

Women in many states were eagerly voting in local elections.

The more Catt heard these arguments, the harder she worked to disprove them. She often used her opponents' own arguments against them. She said that the world needed to make the most of its resources and free the women to help make things right. Even so, her hard work in New York did not pay off that year. The suffragists presented a petition to politicians urging them to add women's suffrage to the new state constitution. Their petition contained 600,000 signatures. The opposition presented a petition with only 15,000 signatures against suffrage. Yet the politicians ignored the suffragists' petition and accepted the petition of the opposing side.

Later in 1894, the fight for suffrage moved to Kansas. Catt was hopeful because Kansas had a strong suffrage organization. Furthermore, Kansas women already voted in city and school elections. But there was a great deal of political unrest. All three major political parties—Republicans, Democrats, and Populists—wanted more power. None of the parties wanted to support women's suffrage out of fear of losing voters for that reason.

Catt was determined. She spoke in all but two of Kansas' 105 counties. Once, she found that the stagecoach was not running, but that didn't stop her. She tried to hire a private driver for another coach but found she couldn't afford it. Finally, she asked if she could pay to take the team of horses for the day and return it the next. Catt rode alone for four hours across Kansas without seeing a soul. The roads were so untraveled that they were hard to see in the tall prairie grass. Catt wondered if she was lost, but she finally arrived at her destination. Local audiences were stunned that a woman had made that journey alone.

Unfortunately, Catt's determination and strength

of character were not enough to help Kansas women that year. Many months of campaigning in Kansas left the suffrage leaders and its treasury exhausted. Catt remembered it as "the most heart-breaking defeat of the suffrage struggle."

Catt returned to her home to rest after the ordeal in Kansas. When she was depressed, Catt liked to garden and cook. She also enjoyed canning vegetables. As she cooked and worked around the house, she planned future campaigns and how to prepare for them.

In January 1895, Catt set off again for a tour of

Catt enjoyed reading and spent some of her free time in her library at home.

the Southern states with Susan B. Anthony. The suffragists had not worked in the South before. They knew it would be tough because many Southerners saw the suffragists simply as strong-minded women from the East who knew nothing of their lives and struggles. Still, the suffragists held meetings in Kentucky, Tennessee, Louisiana, and Alabama.

The tour ended in Atlanta for the 1895 national NAWSA convention. As Catt observed Anthony, she worried about the organization depending so heavily on the leadership of one aging woman. Therefore, in her report, Catt proposed major organizational changes in the structure of the group. She said that they would no longer be introducing people to the idea of suffrage. Instead, they were on to the next step. This next step required a carefully planned policy.

In her plan, Catt wanted to form and lead an organization committee that would manage a budget of $5,000 a year, coordinate Southern and Western state campaigns, and build suffrage clubs that would last beyond each campaign.

Another part of her plan was to educate women on political issues. Catt felt this would help keep the attention of not only local suffrage clubs but that of members in states where suffrage had already been won. Catt wanted to hire a group to begin this educational plan. She also suggested instruction that focused on equality between men and women.

Catt also proposed that suffragists be very visible and attend all county and state political conventions. She wanted them to make themselves known to all office holders and candidates. Catt said that doing so would convince the politicians that women were valuable voters. She wanted the press to constantly be given suffrage updates. She also wanted a finance committee formed to provide funds for the work that needed to be done.

Susan B. Anthony understood that Catt's plan meant changes for the organization. Anthony knew she was aging and that she needed to hand control over to someone who could take the cause to the next level. Though it would be five years before Catt became president, she was already very much in control of NAWSA's direction, for the group accepted her suggestions at the 1895 convention.

Once Catt got her plans in place, she began the practical work. She had other suffragists compile lists of property taxes paid by women. She wanted to show politicians that in paying taxes, women had equal responsibilities but were still not allowed equal rights. Catt thought that anyone who supported the Declaration of Independence would also support women's suffrage.

Catt spent much of 1895 working for the Organization Committee and sorting out the records

A female president speaks to a crowd in a turn-of-the-century political cartoon.

of NAWSA, which were a mess. She found that some states hadn't recorded the names of any suffragists, and some clubs hadn't lasted after they'd been organized. Catt also sorted through notes and

> *Throughout these years, George Catt was very supportive of his wife. He was generous with time and money. He truly admired Carrie's work and dedication. George wanted women's suffrage as much as his wife did. In order to increase membership, the Catts even offered their own money as incentive.*

correspondence that dated back many years.

In the fall of 1895, Catt made a seven-state trip to the West. She believed those states had good reason to hope for women's suffrage. One state Catt did not visit was Utah. She felt she didn't know enough about the state to do any good. Instead, she left suffrage in the hands of Emmeline B. Wells, a member of the Organization Committee. Wells was successful in her campaign, and in 1896, Utah became the third state to grant women's suffrage.

Both Idaho and California had suffrage referendums on the ballots that same year, but the suffragists chose to focus their efforts in California. Catt traveled the state for two months with other suffragists. The press was friendly to them. Catt later recalled the campaign as the "best conducted, liveliest and most enthusiastic" of her experience. But four days before the election, several newspapers in northern California cities printed very negative editorials about the suffragists. Catt and others believed the newspapers had been paid to publish negative articles by those with liquor interests.

The suffrage referendum in California didn't pass, but it did in Idaho. Catt had stopped in Idaho on her way to California in August. She spoke at each political party's convention and got each party to endorse women's suffrage. Idaho went on to become the fourth state to grant women the right to vote.

With a spirit that never quit, Catt continued to work with determination and enthusiasm. In the next few years, she ran campaigns all over the country. She organized new clubs, lobbied politicians for support, and raised money. Catt took her work very seriously. Even though the suffrage movement would have no victories for 14 years after Idaho, Catt continued to be positive and encouraging. The movement depended on both her leadership and her optimism. ❧

5 PRESIDENT OF NAWSA

❦

In 1900, Susan B. Anthony turned 80. The other three original leaders had already died. Anthony knew it was time for new leadership in the movement. Three women were considered good candidates: Anna Howard Shaw, Lillie Devereaux Blake, and Carrie Chapman Catt.

Shaw was an active suffragist and supporter of Anthony. She was a motivating speaker and hard worker. There were reasons, however, to not elect her. Many felt she lacked the organizational and leadership qualities necessary to be president. Furthermore, she was unmarried and needed a salary to support herself. Finally, Shaw had been connected to the temperance movement, a movement that often hurt the suffrage agenda.

Carrie Chapman Catt followed her mentor, Susan B. Anthony, as president of the NAWSA.

A doctor by pro-fession, Anna Howard Shaw was also the first female Methodist min-ister in the United States.

Lillie Blake also was a dedicated supporter and good speaker. She had been president of the New York State Suffrage Association. She lacked the national recognition, however, that Catt had earned.

Many people encouraged Catt to run for president, including Alice Stone Blackwell, Lucy Stone's daughter. Lucy Stone had said on her deathbed that she hoped everyone would vote for Catt if she ever ran for president of the national organization. Alice remembered that and strongly supported Catt.

Carrie Chapman Catt did not want to run for president. She didn't want all the responsibility added to her work in the Organization Committee. She didn't want to be away from home so much, and she didn't feel she could afford it financially. George advised her to take the job and said not to worry about the money. The two of them knew that in reality, Catt had been leading the movement for some time, quietly standing behind Anthony. It was time for the actual leader to step forward and become the official leader.

At the national convention in Washington in February, Lillie Blake withdrew her name. Catt's election to the presidency was almost unanimous. She earned 254 of 275 votes. Anthony announced how pleased she was and acknowledged all of Catt's contributions to the suffrage movement.

The next day, Catt experienced her first bump in the presidential road. She was surprised that NAWSA's Executive Committee wanted to dissolve the Organization Committee that she had headed for the previous five years. Members feared Catt would become too powerful as both president of the national organization and chairperson of the Organization Committee.

After the vote to do away with the Organization Committee, Catt locked herself in her room, threw herself on her bed, and cried. She considered resigning from the presidency. She knew better, however. Catt knew that jealousy, bad talk, and slander could destroy an organization, and she did not want that to happen to NAWSA. She believed with all of her heart that the nation needed women as voters.

Catt's first year as president of NAWSA was much like the previous several years of her life. She went on a spring tour, visiting Tennessee, Arkansas, and Mississippi. Following that, she went on to Ohio and Massachusetts, trying to boost membership and attendance at meetings and conventions. She knew that NAWSA needed extra help that year, 1900, because there was another presidential election between Republican William McKinley and Democrat William Jennings Bryan, who had faced each other four years earlier.

NAWSA asked to speak at both parties' conventions in August 1900. The Republicans gave the group only 10 minutes, and the Democrats didn't give them any time at all. None of the

William Jennings Bryan was a strong supporter of women's suffrage. Though he was not elected to the presidency, his leadership on this issue helped the suffragists keep the conversation about suffrage going at the highest levels of government. Today, Bryan is most-remembered for his prosecution of the famed 1925 "Scopes Monkey Trial," in which a Tennessee schoolteacher was put on trial for teaching about evolution.

politicians wanted to add suffrage to their issues for fear of losing voters.

In response to being shut out, Catt had an idea. She organized a national suffrage bazaar in New York City's Madison Square Garden, which featured goods from the home state of each suffrage association. Louisiana sold figs, pecans, pralines, molasses, and sugarcane. Utah sold bales of native silk. Florida sold citrus fruits and alligators. Idaho sold Native American artifacts. Kansas sold flour and butter. Iowa contributed a carload of pigs. There was food, entertainment, and educational programs dedicated to suffrage. Many people attended the bazaar. At the end of the week, NAWSA had earned $10,000—an astonishing amount in those days.

Once she was president of NAWSA, Catt could more easily pursue some of her other ideas for women's suffrage. Ever since the Congress of Women in 1893, Catt had been thinking over the idea of an international suffrage organization. She knew that the largest women's organization in the world was the International Council of Women (ICW), which had membership in the millions. The ICW supported many reforms such as education, peace, dress reform, and clean streets. Catt knew that suffrage was not the ICW's main concern, but she wanted to join with them.

When Catt approached Susan B. Anthony with

the idea of starting an organization to support worldwide suffrage efforts, Anthony was not enthusiastic. Catt was surprised, but she hadn't known that Anthony and Stanton had started the ICW in 1888. They did so to work on women's suffrage but abandoned it when some leading English women refused to support the cause. Anthony said Catt could go ahead but that she was on her own.

Catt decided to take up international women's suffrage herself. Her first task was to create questionnaires and send them to female leaders all over the world. The questions were about women's rights in each country. Catt wanted to know about jobs and wages for women, restrictions put on women, and divorce and custody rights. She got responses from 32 countries. After that, Catt decided to meet with representatives from as many countries as possible. She planned the meeting for the same time when the 1902 NAWSA convention would be taking place in Washington, D.C.

Representatives from around the world attended the meeting. There were women from Great Britain, Germany, Norway, Sweden, and Denmark. Delegates also arrived from Chile, Turkey, Hungary, Russia, and Switzerland. With Catt's determination, the International Woman Suffrage Alliance (IWSA) was formed in 1902. She would stay committed to the organization for the rest of her life.

Later in 1902, Catt turned her focus back to suffrage efforts at home, traveling to New Hampshire to lend her support to the suffrage movement there. She knew that the area was conservative and that there was little hope of getting women's suffrage passed. Still, the determined Catt organized meetings, speakers, and workers. It was the coldest winter she could remember. Speakers traveled the state in horse-drawn sleighs, covered with heavy woolen blankets and with hot bricks at their feet. They campaigned hard and long, but the amendment lost by more than 9,000 votes. Though she was upset by the loss, Catt stayed positive by telling herself and others that they'd done the best they could.

Catt had only three or four days at home before setting off to the NAWSA convention held in March 1903. There, many noticed that Catt looked thin and pale. It was her fourth year as NAWSA president, and she had been working hard for years. She was exhausted and needed a rest. She not only suffered from debilitating headaches, but she was also concerned for her husband, whose stomach was giving him trouble.

The Catts took a European vacation, traveling together through Italy, France, and Switzerland. The trip was good for Carrie, but George's condition did not improve. Soon after, they sold their Brooklyn home and moved to Manhattan.

Catt decided to resign as NAWSA president so she could care for herself and her husband. In the January 1904 issue of the *Woman's Journal,* she wrote:

> ... *I shall not stand for reelection to the presidency of the National American Woman Suffrage Association at the coming convention in Washington. ... I have no intention of retiring from suffrage work, although I find that rest from the responsibilities of the office [has] become necessary. This alone is my reason for wishing to withdraw my name at this*

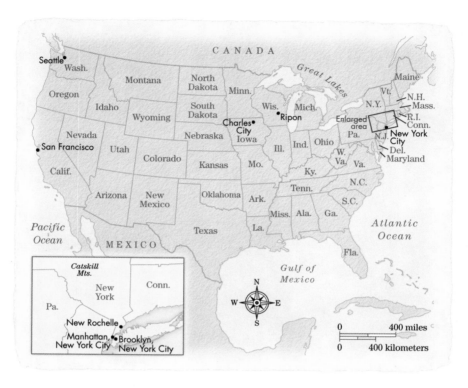

Carrie Chapman Catt lived in many different regions of the United States during her lifetime.

time. Whatever strength or ability I may have is first, last, and all the time consecrated to this cause, which is dearer than all others to me.

After Catt's resignation, Anna Howard Shaw was elected the new president of NAWSA. Catt agreed to serve as her vice president. ✤

6 INTERNATIONAL WORK

After Catt resigned as NAWSA's president, she was able to pursue her interests in the International Woman Suffrage Alliance. Most of the work could be done from her home, although she sometimes attended conventions and meetings.

The 1904 IWSA meeting was held in Berlin, Germany. At this convention were women from several different countries, creating a very diverse group. This meant that Catt needed to use great skill and diplomacy in her speeches. Many members were not familiar with parliamentary procedure, which the Americans followed closely. But by carefully explaining herself and her methods, Catt won the hearts of the world's women. She was clear and kind. She presented a gavel from the women of

England's suffragettes often brought attention to their cause with activities that led to their being restrained or jailed.

Wyoming, who had enjoyed full voting rights longer than any women in the world. Members were amused when Catt told them that customs inspectors suspected the gavel was a weapon.

In four days, IWSA members reaffirmed the 1902 declaration, approved a constitution, established a member list, and elected officers. They had no common language, so all speeches had to be translated. All the women who attended the Berlin convention went home with new ideas and new friends. Catt remembered the excitement of those early IWSA meetings for the rest of her life.

Catt spent most of 1904 and 1905 caring for her husband. George suffered from gallstones, a condition in which calcium deposits form in the gall bladder. He was very weak and often in great pain. Catt limited her travel and declined reelection to the vice presidency of NAWSA in June 1904. She lectured on the evolution of the women's movement and spent most of the money she earned on specialists for her headaches. Unfortunately, nothing seemed to

A crowd of women assembled behind the speaker's platform at the opening of the 1904 IWSA convention in Berlin, Germany.

relieve them.

In the fall of 1905, George had a final attack of gallstone pain. When doctors operated to remove the gallstones, they found that George also had a bleeding ulcer. He got an infection and later died on October 8, 1905.

Catt was devastated by the death of her husband. For weeks, she lost all interest in suffrage and everything else. She couldn't cope with reminders of him around their apartment. She rented rooms in a hotel and asked her friend Mary Hay to stay with her.

After a time, Catt moved back home, and Mary moved in with her. They were good friends and roommates, both dedicated to suffrage. Catt was popular and outgoing—good at dealing with crowds and organizations. Mary was more successful at behind-the-scenes work. Their arrangement so suited both of them that they lived together until Mary's death many years later.

Catt went to Denmark in 1906 for the third annual IWSA conference. Some women from England's Women's Social and Political Union (WSPU) were present. This suffrage group had been using tactics that resulted in some of them being jailed. Their strategy was to shock and frustrate the officials into overreacting. Then the women would publicize the oppression. These women were called "suffragettes" in the press to distinguish them from the more mild-mannered "suffragists."

Although Catt admired the suffragettes' zeal, the IWSA generally worked toward its goals peacefully. Some IWSA members felt the WSPU suffragettes hurt the British suffrage movement. Others admired their ability to get press coverage. In the end, however, the IWSA did not allow the WSPU to join on the grounds that another British branch of ISWA already existed.

Despite the presence of the WSPU, the 1906 conference was a success. It motivated delegates to work for suffrage in their own countries. Finland had already gained suffrage since the 1904 meeting in Berlin, and Norway would have women's suffrage within three years' time. Danish women were soon allowed to vote in city elections. Catt traveled to Hungary and Austria after the conference to help the movement in those countries. American women were encouraged by all the progress in Europe. No new suffrage amendments had been passed in the United States since Idaho in 1896.

In 1907, Catt lost two more loved ones. Both her mother, Maria, and her brother Will died that year. Catt had gone home to Charles City to care for her mother prior to her death. She stayed in Iowa to grieve for the next two months. In a letter to a friend, she compared her grief at these losses to that which she felt when George had died two years earlier: "I am quite normal mentally, which is a great improvement over my condition two years ago. Then I felt sure I could not live long and I was not at all interested in whether I did or not."

By the end of February 1908, Catt was ready to get back to work. She spoke in support of

> *After losing George, Catt had to deal with yet another loss. Susan B. Anthony died in March 1906 after suffering from pneumonia. Catt was filled with an intense grief at the loss of her mentor, who had spent her life working so tirelessly for the cause.*

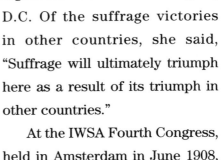

A number of countries granted women suffrage before the United States. New Zealand was the first, in 1893, followed by Australia, Finland, Norway, Denmark, the Soviet Union, England, Germany, the Netherlands, and Canada. In the following 100 years, women received the right to vote in almost every country where men had the right.

suffrage at congressional hearings in New York and Washington, D.C. Of the suffrage victories in other countries, she said, "Suffrage will ultimately triumph here as a result of its triumph in other countries."

At the IWSA Fourth Congress, held in Amsterdam in June 1908, Catt continued with that theme. She said that the woman's movement could not be considered a success until woman's history became part of the world's history. At the conference, European delegates reported success, and women came from as far away as South Africa and Australia. There was even a male delegate from Great Britain's Men's League for Women's Enfranchisement. The conference got excellent press coverage, and Catt was pleased.

By the time the 1909 IWSA conference met in London, Catt's health had been declining for some time. Therefore, she attended few events and talked with fewer people than she ever had at a meeting. She had suffered from migraine headaches for years, and she also had anemia, a condition of low iron levels in the blood. She was weak and tired.

Following doctor's orders, Catt rested in New York's Catskill Mountains for the summer of 1909. Unfortunately, her health did not improve. In June 1910, she underwent an operation, after which her doctor said she should rest a full year. Catt told her doctor about the responsibilities that made such rest impossible, and he responded, "Then you must rest two years, instead of one."

Catt set sail with Mary Hay in April 1911 in order to attend the Sixth Conference of the IWSA in Stockholm, Sweden. At the June conference, Catt spoke of the worldwide movement of women into the workplace. She pointed out that women worked alongside men but did not earn nearly the same wages.

After the conference, Catt traveled the world. She was supposed to be resting but could not leave her cause out of her travels. She took a 76-day trip to Africa, during which she made 45 speeches. Clearly, she was not resting as much as her doctors would have liked.

While in Africa, Catt met Mohandas Gandhi, an Indian man who would lead a massive civil rights movement in India in years to come. At this time, Catt learned that California had passed a law allowing women to vote. She was thrilled, knowing how important California's success was to the other states in the West.

M.K.GANDHI.
ATTORNEY.

Indian Mohandas Gandhi (center) met Catt while practicing as an attorney in South Africa.

Catt headed to other continents and countries where she asked many questions of the people she met. She was curious about the veils Muslim women wore and noted that Middle Eastern women weren't given much of an education. She observed slave conditions in what is now Sri Lanka. When she was told the tea pickers were happy with their lifestyles, she responded that she had heard the same about the contentment of wives, but only as spoken by their husbands.

In India, Catt met a few women trying to bring social change to India. These women were fighting to end child marriages, increase education for women, and improve women's wages.

Catt also visited China, where she found that women were in high positions in rebel groups. She also found an active women's rights group in Shanghai. Theirs became the first group from the Far East to join IWSA.

Throughout her trip, Catt met all kinds of women with all kinds of differing needs. Yet she couldn't help but notice that all the women wanted one thing: They wanted a better way of life for themselves and their daughters.

Catt stopped in London on her way to Budapest, Hungary, for the 1913 IWSA meeting. She learned that the suffragettes there were lighting fires, breaking windows, and staging hunger strikes to get their way. The British government ordered that those on hunger strikes be tube fed and forced to get nutrition. Catt was both thrilled by the power of the movement there and frightened by the violence.

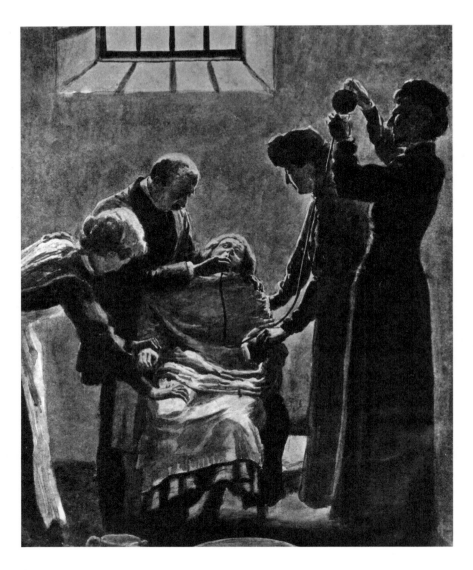

Suffragettes on hunger strikes were often force-fed with a long tube down their throats.

She worried that the people opposing the suffragettes were opposed more to the criminal acts than to suffrage itself. In the *Woman's Journal*, Catt wrote, "The suffrage campaign in the United States is a dull and commonplace affair when compared with the sizzling white heat of the British struggle."

At the conference in Budapest, Catt resigned as president of IWSA. She needed to give her energy to the New York campaign back home. New York was both the hope and despair of the suffrage movement. It was the home of the movement and had a huge membership, but it also was the place that had the strongest opposition. That opposition included conservative thinkers, politicians who feared women becoming too powerful, and those involved with the liquor industry.

Though she knew it was an uphill battle, Catt came up with a plan for the New York campaign that resulted in New York City's Woman Suffrage Party membership growing to more than 100,000 people. The high point of the campaign was a parade that drew more than 1.5 million spectators. About 30,000 women—and 5,000 men—marched up Fifth Avenue in the bitter cold.

Even though the suffragists held more than 10,000 meetings in the six months before the

The IWSA conference in Budapest was the largest yet. More than 2,800 people attended, and news reporters from around the world were there to cover the events. But the 1913 conference would be the last the IWSA held for a while. Many European countries were soon caught up in World War I. The women's suffrage movement in Europe was put on hold as people dealt with the impact of war.

*New York City
suffragists
carried a
ballot box
on a stretcher
in a 1915 suf-
frage parade.*

election—even though they printed 7.5 million leaflets and raised $95,000—the vote for the amendment lost by more than 194,000 votes.

New York's neighbors in New Jersey, Massachusetts, and Pennsylvania also were denied

women's suffrage that year. NAWSA's president, Anna Howard Shaw, remarked that night that opponents were saying this loss would set the suffragists back 10 years. She asked Catt how long it would delay Catt's fight. Catt replied, "Only until we can get a little sleep. Our campaign will be on again tomorrow morning— and forever until we get the vote." Women's suffrage had earned more than a million votes in four states, and politicians could not ignore numbers like that. Catt knew victory would be coming.

Two days later, the New York campaign began afresh. Supporters were so enthusiastic that $10,000 was raised on the spot. Catt called on the suffragists again: "Roll up your sleeves, set your mind to making history and wage such a fight for liberty that the whole world will respect our sex." 🐲

7 THE FEDERAL AMENDMENT CAMPAIGN

Chapter

೧೯೨೦

In December 1915, the United States Senate and the House of Representatives introduced a bill that would add women's suffrage to the U.S. Constitution. This federal amendment, called the Anthony Amendment in honor of Susan B. Anthony, was an opportunity for the suffragists to fight like they'd never fought before. Anna Howard Shaw didn't think she had it in her to carry out this huge undertaking. She resigned as NAWSA president, agreeing to stay on as a speaker.

Many members wanted Catt to replace Shaw, but Catt did not want the position. She wanted to keep focusing exclusively on New York. In the end, however, Catt accepted the presidency. In 1916, South Dakota, Iowa, and West Virginia were all

Carrie Chapman Catt marched in support of women's suffrage in a New York City parade.

In 1910, the *American Ladies' Tailors Association* introduced a special outfit created for the suffragists. This "suffragette suit" included a skirt that was divided down the middle, much like loose pants. Many suffragists wore these suits when they campaigned or marched in support of their cause. The skirts allowed them to move more freely and with greater comfort.

voting on suffrage. Catt campaigned as much as she could in those states. Still, South Dakota was a repeat of years earlier. Many foreign-born people who were not yet citizens voted, and suffrage was defeated. In Iowa, suffrage lost because of the liquor interests and dishonest election officials. In fact, a report later indicated that 47 violations of Iowa's election laws had been committed. And in West Virginia, female poll workers reported that drunken men showed up in high numbers to vote against the women. Suffrage lost there, too.

Catt knew that with the U.S. presidential election coming that fall, she needed to have a women's suffrage policy on each political party's platform. She faced a lot of resistance, however. Lobbyists for the liquor industry continued to convince politicians that a vote for suffrage would mean a vote for prohibition. In the conservative East, politicians seemed to be living in the past and would not vote for change. In the South, politicians did not want to vote for anything that would take away the power of white men.

Catt knew that they needed a good plan. She instructed the NAWSA Congressional Committee to write a proposal asking each political party to endorse women's suffrage. She had suffragists lobby hard to get politicians to agree to include suffrage proposals and then got women in every state and voting district to pester them to keep their word. Suffragists from the national association planned rallies in Chicago and St. Louis, where the political

Schoolgirls created posters with women's equality themes for a suffrage poster contest.

party conventions would be held.

Although each political party finally added suffrage to their platform, it wasn't the success Catt had hoped for. The Progressive Party openly supported women's suffrage, but they were not a very powerful party. The Republicans issued a statement that said they favored the extension of suffrage to women but recognized that each state has the right to settle the question individually. The Democratic Party issued a similar statement at its June convention.

Catt was deeply disappointed, and she was concerned with the morale of NAWSA, which had experienced one defeat after another. She and her executive committee called an emergency convention in September 1916. The goal of the convention was to decide whether to 1) drop work on the federal amendment and concentrate on state legislatures; 2) drop work on the state legislatures and only work on the federal amendment; or 3) continue working for a federal amendment through the state legislatures.

Catt spoke and insisted on the third option. She fully believed that the federal amendment would only get passed through total cooperation from the states and that the time to do it was right now. She wanted a simultaneous campaign to be carried out in all 48 states. Nothing less than nationwide, nonstop campaigning would do.

In the spring of 1917, after Germany continued to torpedo American merchant ships in the Atlantic Ocean, the United States entered World War I. Catt knew the war would have a negative effect on the suffrage movement, but she felt she had no choice but to support the war. When President Wilson asked her to be part of the Women's Committee of the Council of National Defense, Catt accepted.

The Women's Committee of the Council of National Defense helped address the food shortage in the United States that was a result of the war. The Women's Committee started a program to help women plant vegetable gardens across the country. They printed recipes for meatless, butterless, and wheatless meals. They got women to knit socks, make bandages, and work in factories. Women who took on factory work still needed help at home, so the Women's Committee encouraged other

In 1917, a suffragist named Alice Paul arranged for women to picket the White House around the clock in order to get the attention of President Woodrow Wilson. In June 1917, a mob attacked the picketers. Many people were arrested, and more than 200 women faced trial. In jail, the women were treated poorly and given wormy food. Some were even beaten by their guards. News of this treatment horrified many people and helped create more support for the suffragists. In November 1917, President Wilson ordered the women set free. He urged senators to pass a suffrage amendment. Picketing continued for the next three years, even during the war.

women to open day-care centers and to help in the schools. Catt traveled for the organization, meeting with government officials and representatives of labor groups, as well as with suffragists around the country.

Catt saw the remarkable work that women were

During World War I, many women worked in factories making materials for the war.

doing in wartime and urged Congress to pass a federal suffrage amendment as a war measure. But Congress refused to discuss any bills or issues except those relating to the war. In retaliation, Catt organized a massive campaign in New York, where the suffrage party's strength and numbers had continued to grow under Mary Hay's leadership. Catt led a march just before the fall 1917 elections. Petitions in support of women's suffrage contained more than a million signatures. On election day, the New York state suffrage amendment finally passed.

Catt and the other suffragists were thrilled. Years of hard work in New York had finally paid off. In addition, women in North Dakota, Indiana, Michigan, Ohio, Nebraska, and Rhode Island won the right to vote in presidential elections, while Vermont women won the right to vote in city elections. The suffragists were making progress after years of defeat.

At NAWSA's December 1917 national convention in Washington, D.C., many of the state leaders reported that their states would soon support women's suffrage. Catt said, "There is one thing mightier than kings or armies, congresses or political parties—the power of an idea when its time has come to move." She wanted more than anything to push the federal amendment through Congress, and she felt certain that victory was near.

World War I ended in Europe in 1918, but the fight for women's suffrage continued. Women from every state camped out in Washington, D.C. They took turns lobbying at the Capitol. Every politician who walked by had to hear the suffragists' message.

Catt felt the women's continuous presence was necessary because the road to passing a federal amendment was long. First, each branch of Congress had to debate and vote on the amendment. If it passed in both the House and Senate, it then needed to be ratified by three-fourths of the states.

In January 1918, the House of Representatives passed the Anthony Amendment with the needed two-thirds majority. The Senate, however, rejected the amendment by two votes. Early in 1919, it failed again in the Senate by one vote. In May, the House again passed the amendment and in June, the Senate followed suit. Catt had stayed home the day of

The U.S. Constitution can be amended in two ways. In the first, two-thirds of the states call for a convention, similar to the one that first created the Constitution in 1787. Any amendments suggested at the convention then have to be ratified by three-quarters of the states. In the other amendment method, a member of the Congress proposes an amendment, and two-thirds of the lawmakers in both the House of Representatives and Senate must then approve it. After this approval, the amendment goes to the states to be ratified. This amendment method is the only one that has been used.

the Senate vote to avoid the senators' speeches, but her friend Mary Hay called her with the good news. Catt was thrilled.

The final hurdle before the amendment could be passed was that it needed to be ratified by the states. Because of Catt's efforts, each state already had a ratification committee in place even before the suffrage amendment had reached Congress. Catt immediately sent telegrams to each state's ratification committee. She said that if their legislators were in session, she wanted to see ratification immediately.

Suffragists looked on as Missouri governor Frederick D. Garner ratified the 19th Amendment.

And she did. Both Wisconsin and Illinois ratified the amendment within the week. They were quickly followed by Michigan, Kansas, New York, and Ohio. Pennsylvania, Massachusetts, and Texas ratified the amendment within the month. Before the end of the summer, 17 of the necessary 36 states had ratified the suffrage amendment.

Catt was careful to advise the suffragists to only let the amendment come to a vote in states where they were certain it had enough support to be approved. She knew from experience that victory in one state often led to victory in another and that any defeat would stall the passing. Catt went on a "Wake Up America" tour in October 1919, lobbying harder than ever before. She traveled to 13 states in eight weeks, pushing for ratification with the state legislators.

The fall of 1919 brought with it ratification in five more states, and nine additional states ratified the amendment in early 1920. Some states were strongly opposed, particularly in the South. The amendment initially failed in Alabama, Delaware, Georgia, Mississippi, South Carolina, and Virginia.

In February 1920, Catt decided to hold a Victory Convention in Chicago. There, she introduced the idea of an organization that would teach women about politics and voting. This group, called the League of Women Voters, would be an independent educational organization and would not support any specific political party. The League of Women Voters still exists today.

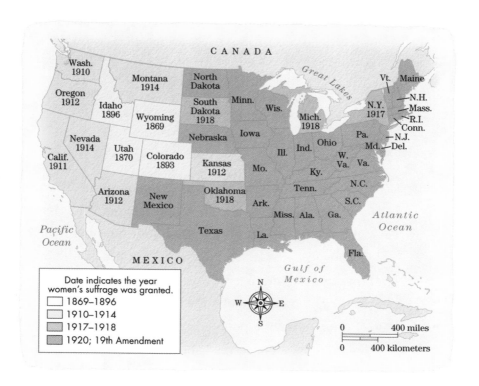

Date indicates the year women's suffrage was granted.
- 1869–1896
- 1910–1914
- 1917–1918
- 1920; 19th Amendment

Nevertheless, the suffragists felt confident they would eventually reach their goal.

The suffragists needed only one more state to finally ratify the 19th Amendment. Catt and other suffragists headed to Tennessee, ready for a fight. It was a good thing they were ready, too, because it was a nasty battle. Catt wrote:

Suffrage was granted to American women over the course of 51 years.

> *In the short time I have been in Tennessee's capital, I have been called more names, been ... more lied about than*

in the thirty previous years I worked for suffrage. I was flooded with anonymous letters, vulgar, ignorant, insane. Strange men and groups of men sprang up, men we had never met before in battle. ... They ... tapped our telephones, listened outside our windows. ... They attacked our private and public lives.

On the day of the vote, the resolution was initially tied 48 to 48. Then, a 24-year-old first-term representative from the mountains of a rural county changed his vote from "against" to "for." He did so because his mother had wanted him to vote for the suffrage amendment. The young man, Harry T. Burns, knew the people in the area he represented were mostly not in favor of the amendment, but he changed his vote anyway. Burns was a hero to the suffragists because his switch meant victory. Ratification was complete.

On August 26, 1920, the 19th Amendment to the U.S. Constitution was passed, finally granting American women the right to vote. Catt said,

This is a glorious and wonderful day. Now that we have the vote, let us remember that we are no longer petitioners. We are not the wards of the nation but free and equal citizens. Let us do our part to keep it a true and triumphant democracy.

Catt had spent more than 40 years of her life working toward this day. She and the rest of the suffrage leaders were eager to take full advantage of their hard-won right. ℘

Carrie Chapman Catt (left) and Mary Hay cast their votes in the 1920 presidential election.

Chapter

8 FINDING PEACE

❧〜❧

While the 19th Amendment ended the women's suffrage struggle in the United States, that struggle continued in countries around the world. World War I had put the suffrage cause on hold in Europe. Once the war was over, resuming the IWSA was difficult because of the bitter feelings between European countries. Catt had her work cut out for her.

Catt wanted IWSA to work toward universal adult suffrage throughout the world. She wanted women everywhere to be a united political front that worked toward social reform and peace. To go about this, she felt she needed to bring in the countries not represented in IWSA. Therefore, she set up committees to research women's issues in those countries.

After women had been granted suffrage, Carrie Chapman Catt focused her efforts on eliminating war and securing peace in the world.

Catt was especially curious about the status of women in South America because it was the only continent that didn't allow women to vote. She planned a Pan-American conference with Lavinia Engle from Baltimore, Maryland. The women at the conference set up a new alliance called the Pan-American Association for the Advancement of Women. Carrie Chapman Catt was the first president and kept her post for one year.

During that year, Catt co-authored a book about the history of the suffrage movement in the United States. She and Nettie Shuler wrote *Woman Suffrage and Politics: The Inner Story of the Suffrage Movement.* As she wrote about the history of suffrage, she was able to deal with some of her lingering anger about the opposition's dishonesty in trying to prevent women's suffrage all those years.

By 1925, Catt had committed herself to world peace. She felt she had done her share for suffrage and wanted to do what she could to promote peace in the world. In 1925, she led the first meeting of the Committee on the Cause and Cure of War in Washington, D.C. The committee's primary goals included educating people about peace and negotiating nonmilitary solutions when countries disagreed. The committee lobbied Congress to pursue peaceful solutions with other countries.

Catt served as president of the committee from

1925 through 1932. She openly voiced her opinion that war solved nothing, destroyed much, and should become a thing of the past. During her years as leader, the committee avoided dwelling on past wars and instead tried to find ways to end the economic and political reasons for war. Many political and social groups disagreed with the committee and its approach, but Catt carried on until the age of 69, when she was ready to retire.

She bought a house in New Rochelle, New York, which was a 30-minute train ride from New York

Catt (right) attended a banquet for the Committee on the Cause and Cure of War with future first lady Eleanor Roosevelt.

City. Mary Hay moved in with her into the house, which was large and airy. It had sunrooms, a library, and a large living room. Catt hung her collection of letters, documents, and photos from the suffrage movement on the walls.

Sadly, Catt and Mary didn't get to enjoy their retirement together for very long. Catt had planned a big party to celebrate Mary's 71st birthday, on August 29, 1928. The two women were dressing for the party when Catt noticed that Mary's chatter in the next room had stopped. Catt found Mary unconscious on the bed. She died a few hours later from what doctors said was a burst blood vessel in the brain. Catt was shocked.

After Mary's funeral, Catt's friend Alda Wilson came to stay with her and ended up moving in permanently. Catt filled the void left by Mary with trips, meetings, and visits. Alda tried to get Catt to slow down, but Catt wouldn't have it.

At this stage of her life, Catt's main concern was world peace. When World War II started in 1939, she served as the honorary chair of the Women's Action Committee for Victory and Lasting Peace. Part of Catt's work during the war involved helping Jewish people who suffered as a result of Germany's Nazi regime. From the study of her New Rochelle home, she wrote letters to important people in Europe. She wrote press releases, pamphlets, and resolutions.

Catt started petitions to help Jewish people living in exile. She also was among the first to inform the U.S. government about how Jewish people were treated in concentration camps and in the ghetto of Warsaw, Poland. Catt lost several friends to the horrors of the concentration camps, where millions of Jews were killed. For her work on behalf of Jewish people, Catt

Children were confined behind barbed wire in the Nazi concentration camp at Auschwitz, in southern Poland.

was awarded the American Hebrew Medal, which was given to those who helped promote understanding between Christians and Jews. It was the first time the medal had been given to a woman.

By the time World War II ended, Carrie Chapman Catt was in her mid-80s. She enjoyed spending time in her library and receiving visitors. She traveled when she was up to it. Catt had spent her whole life

This cartoon honors Carrie Chapman Catt as a "Wonder Woman of History."

working to help others. She had certainly earned the tiny sliver of peace she allowed herself in old age.

On March 8, 1947, Catt spent an ordinary day reading, writing, and talking with a friend who had paid her a visit. Some time after midnight, she suffered a heart attack. Alda Wilson called Catt's doctor, who arrived just before she died at 3:30 A.M.

Catt had said she wanted a simple funeral, so hers was held in her living room with about 60 people. They included mostly friends from her suffrage and peace work. Catt was later buried alongside her friend Mary Hay at Woodlawn Cemetery. Just after Mary had died, Catt had a gravestone monument erected. It read: "Here lie two, united in friendship for 38 years through constant service to a great cause."

Catt's life was indeed one of constant service. Through her organization, commitment, and service, she helped make suffrage a reality for American women and brought women of the world another step closer to achieving the dream of equality. ❧

CATT'S LIFE

1866

Moves with family
to Charles City, Iowa

1880

Graduates from Iowa
State Agricultural
College in Ames
(now Iowa State
University)

1859

Born January 9 in
Ripon, Wisconsin

1880

1858

English scientist
Charles Darwin
presents his theory
of evolution

1879

Electric lights
are invented

WORLD EVENTS

1883

Appointed first woman superintendent of schools in Mason City, Iowa

1885

Marries Leo Chapman; helps him run the *Mason City Republican*

1886

Moves to San Francisco, California; husband, Leo Chapman, dies

1885

1881

The first Japanese political parties are formed

1886

Grover Cleveland dedicates the Statue of Liberty in New York, a gift from the people of France

CATT'S LIFE

1890

Attends her first
National American
Woman Suffrage
Association (NAWSA)
conference in
Washington, D.C.,
where she lectures
for the first time;
marries George Catt

1900

Succeeds Susan B.
Anthony as president
of NAWSA

1902

Helps form the
International Woman
Suffrage Alliance
(IWSA)

1890

1893

Women gain voting
privileges in New
Zealand, the first
country to take such
a step

1901

The first Nobel Prize
ceremony is held in
Stockholm

WORLD EVENTS

1911

Travels throughout Europe, Africa, and Asia for the suffrage movement

1905

Husband, George Catt, dies; Mary Hay becomes roommate

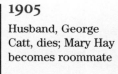

1910

1903

Brothers Orville and Wilbur Wright successfully fly a powered airplane

1914

Archduke Franz Ferdinand is assassinated, launching World War I

CATT'S LIFE

1920

Sees victory when the 19th Amendment to the U.S. Constitution is passed, giving women the right to vote

1915

Becomes NAWSA president again after Anna Howard Shaw resigns

1919

Helps form League of Women Voters

1920

1916

German-born physicist Albert Einstein publishes his general theory of relativity

1922

The tomb of Tutankhamen is discovered by British archaeologist Howard Carter

WORLD EVENTS

1923

Publishes *Woman Suffrage and Politics: The Inner Story of the Suffrage Movement* with Nettie Shuler

1925

Establishes the Committee on the Cause and Cure of War

1947

Dies in New Rochelle, New York, on March 9

1925

1926

A.A. Milne publishes *Winnie the Pooh*

1945

The United Nations is founded

Life at a Glance

DATE OF BIRTH: January 9, 1859

PLACE OF BIRTH: Ripon, Wisconsin

FATHER: Lucius Lane

MOTHER: Maria Clinton Lane

EDUCATION: College degree: Iowa
Agricultural College in
Ames (now Iowa State
University)

FIRST SPOUSE: Leo Chapman (d. 1886)

DATE OF
MARRIAGE: February 12, 1885

SECOND SPOUSE: George Catt (d. 1905)

DATE OF
MARRIAGE: June 10, 1890

CHILDREN: None

DATE OF DEATH: March 9, 1947

PLACE OF BURIAL: Woodlawn Cemetery,
New Rochelle, New York

In the Library

Bausum, Ann. *With Courage and Cloth: Winning the Fight for a Woman's Right to Vote.* Washington: National Geographic, 2004.

Beard, Darleen Bailey. *Operation Clean Sweep.* New York: Farrar, Straus and Giroux, 2004.

Bjornlund, Lydia. *Women of the Suffrage Movement.* San Diego: Lucent Books, 2003.

Burgan, Michael. *The 19th Amendment.* Minneapolis: Compass Point Books, 2006.

Rau, Dana Meachen. *Great Women of the Suffrage Movement.* Minneapolis: Compass Point Books, 2006.

Somervill, Barbara. *Votes for Women: The Story of Carrie Chapman Catt.* Greensboro, N.C.: Morgan Reynolds Publishing, 2003.

Look for more Signature Lives books about this era:

Andrew Carnegie: *Captain of Industry*

Douglas MacArthur: *America's General*

Eleanor Roosevelt: *First Lady of the World*

Elizabeth Cady Stanton: *Social Reformer*

Henry B. Gonzalez: *Congressman of the People*

J. Edgar Hoover: *Controversial FBI Director*

Langston Hughes: *The Voice of Harlem*

ON THE WEB

For more information on *Carrie Chapman Catt*, use FactHound to track down Web sites related to this book.

1. Go to *www.facthound.com*
2. Type in a search word related to this book or this book ID: 0756509912
3. Click on the *Fetch It* button.

FactHound will find the best Web sites for you.

HISTORIC SITES

Women's Rights National Historic Park
136 Fall St.
Seneca Falls, NY 13148
315/568-2991
To learn about extraordinary women and view exhibits and artifacts in the town where the women's movement began

The Women's Museum
3800 Parry Ave.
Dallas, TX 75226
214/915-0860
To see exhibits on how women have shaped the nation's history

activist
someone who takes action in pursuing a political or social end

Constitution
the document stating the basic laws of the United States

lobby
to attempt to persuade a political representative or influential person to support or fight a particular cause

parliamentary procedure
a specific method of running a meeting

petition
a written request signed by many people demanding a particular action from an authority or government

platform
the publicly announced policies and promises of a party seeking election, understood as the basis of its actions should it be elected

prohibition
a movement to prohibit the drinking of alcoholic beverages

ratify
to give formal approval to something

referendum
a vote on a specific issue in a specific area

suffrage
the right to vote in public elections

unions
organized groups of workers set up to improve things such as working conditions, wages, and health benefits

Chapter 1

Page 12, sidebar: Elizabeth Cady Stanton, et al. "The Declaration of Sentiments and Resolutions." In *Women's Rights*. Shasta Gaughen, Ed. Detroit: Greenhaven Press, 2003, p. 17.

Chapter 2

Page 16, line 2: Jacqueline Van Voris. *Carrie Chapman Catt: A Public Life*. New York: Feminist Press at the City University of New York, 1987, p. 5; original source: Mrs. William Dick Sporborg. "Mrs. Catt, Nearing Seventy-Seven, Looks Back on Fifty Years of Service to Women." *New York Herald Tribune*, 5 January 1936.

Page 20, line 13: Ibid. p. 8; original source: *Charles City Intelligence*, 28 June 1877, p. 2.

Chapter 3

Page 28, line 26: *Carrie Chapman Catt: A Public Life*. p. 18; original source: *Woman's Journal*, 9 November 1889, p. 356.

Page 31, line 4: Ibid. p. 20; original source: Carrie Catt. "A Suffrage Team." *Woman Citizen*, 8 September 1923, pp. 11–12.

Page 32, line 4: Ibid. p. 23; original source: *New York Times*, 19 March 1911, p. 8.

Page 33, line 3: Ibid. p. 25; original source: Ida Husted Harper. *The Life and Work of Susan B. Anthony, 2*, pp. 693–694.

Page 39, line 5: Ibid. p. 37.

Chapter 4

Page 44, line 4: Carrie Chapman Catt and Nettie Shuler. *Woman Suffrage and Politics: The Inner Story of the Suffrage Movement*, 1923, p. 122. NYC: Scribner's Sons.

Page 48, line 22: *Carrie Chapman Catt: A Public Life*. p. 48.

Chapter 5

Page 58, line 21: Mary Gray Peck. *Carrie Chapman Catt: A Biography*. New York: H.W. Wilson Company, 1944, p. 133; original source: *Woman's Journal*, January 1904.